HOW TO GROW SMALL BUSINESS

The Ultimate Guide to Skyrocketing

Your Business with Strategic Social

Media Marketing and Convert

Followers into Raving Clients

Jerry R. Schaefer

i

OTHER BOOKS BY SAME AUTHOR

1. HOW TO INVEST FOR TEENAGERS
2. HOW TO INVEST $10,000 INTO FINANCIAL FREEDOM
3. HOW TO BUDGET AND SAVE MONEY FOR BEGINNERS
4. THE PATH TO LONG-TERM INVESTMENT
5. FINANCIAL INDEPENDENCE WITH 70% SAVING
6. ONE YEAR TO FINANCIAL FREEDOM
7. INVESTING STRATEGIES FOR ANY BUDGET
8. FROM YOUR FIRST $100K
9. HOW TO INVEST FOR BEGINNERS

TABLE OF CONTENTS

INTRODUCTION

In today's dynamic business landscape, where digital connectivity is the heartbeat of communication, harnessing the power of social media has become imperative for businesses striving for success. This introduction aims to unravel the significance of social media marketing and why it is a game-changer for businesses of all sizes.

The Digital Age and Business Dynamics

We find ourselves in the midst of the Digital Age, where technology not only facilitates but shapes our interactions. Social media platforms have emerged as the nerve centers of this digital revolution, connecting people globally and fundamentally altering the way businesses operate. In this interconnected era, having a robust social media presence is not just an option; it's a necessity.

The Global Marketplace at Your Fingertips

Social media serves as a virtual marketplace, breaking down geographical barriers and providing businesses with unprecedented access to a vast, diverse audience. Whether you're a local coffee shop or an international consultancy firm, social media platforms offer an equal playing field to showcase your brand, products, or services. The ability to reach potential customers worldwide is a monumental shift that traditional marketing methods simply can't match.

Building Brand Visibility and Credibility

Beyond mere visibility, social media allows businesses to craft and control their brand image. It's a dynamic canvas where you can paint the narrative of your business, shaping how your audience perceives you. Consistent, engaging content establishes credibility and fosters a sense of familiarity, making your brand not just a product or service but a story that resonates with your audience.

The Pulse of Your Audience

One of the unparalleled advantages of social media is the real-time feedback loop it provides. Businesses can gauge audience reactions, preferences, and concerns almost instantly. This direct line of communication allows for agile adjustments to strategies, ensuring that your business remains relevant and responsive to the ever-evolving needs of your audience.

Social Proof and Community Building

Social media isn't just about broadcasting; it's about building a community around your brand. Customer testimonials, positive reviews, and user-generated content create social proof, establishing trust and authenticity. A thriving online community not only strengthens your brand but also fosters a sense of belonging among your customers, turning them into loyal advocates.

The Competitive Edge

In a crowded marketplace, standing out is a constant challenge. Social media marketing provides a dynamic platform to showcase your unique value proposition. It's not just about selling a product; it's about telling a compelling story that differentiates you from the competition. Businesses that embrace social media effectively gain a competitive edge by staying top of mind in the digital landscape.

In essence, social media marketing is not merely a tool; it's a transformative force reshaping the business landscape. Its ability to transcend boundaries, amplify brand messages, and foster meaningful connections positions it as a cornerstone for success in the digital era. As we delve deeper into this book, we will unravel the strategies and tactics that will empower you to harness the full potential of social media for your business. Get ready to embark on a journey where your social media presence becomes a catalyst for growth and a key driver of your business success.

The Three Pillars: Lead Generation, Lead Nurture, Lead Conversion

Unlocking the full potential of social media marketing hinges on understanding and effectively implementing the three crucial pillars: Lead Generation, Lead Nurture, and Lead Conversion. These pillars form the backbone of a strategic approach, guiding businesses toward sustainable growth and success in the digital realm.

Lead Generation: Seeding the Future

At the forefront of social media strategy lies Lead Generation – the art of attracting potential customers and initiating the journey from curious onlooker to engaged prospect. In the vast expanse of social media, businesses employ various tactics to capture the attention of their target audience. This could range from creating compelling content and eye-catching visuals to running targeted ads that resonate with specific demographics.

Successful lead generation is not just about quantity; it's about quality. Businesses strive not only to amass leads but to ensure they are relevant and genuinely interested in what the brand has to offer. Social media platforms, with their sophisticated algorithms and data analytics tools, provide businesses with the means to identify and reach potential customers with precision.

Lead Nurture: Cultivating Relationships

Having captured the interest of potential customers, the next step is to cultivate and nurture these leads. Lead Nurture involves building a relationship with your audience through consistent and valuable interactions. This is where businesses move beyond the transactional mindset and focus on providing relevant content that educates, entertains, or solves a problem for their audience.

Lead Nurture is akin to tending to a garden – it requires care, attention, and a strategic approach. By delivering personalized content, responding promptly to inquiries, and guiding leads through a seamless customer journey, businesses can foster a sense of trust and loyalty. The goal is to position your brand as not just a provider of products or services but as a valuable resource that understands and meets the needs of your audience.

Lead Conversion: Turning Interest into Action

The ultimate goal of the social media marketing journey is Lead Conversion – the turning point where a potential customer becomes an actual customer. This step requires a clear and compelling Call to Action (CTA) that guides leads toward making a purchase, signing up for a service, or taking any desired action. Lead Conversion is the culmination of the relationship-building efforts invested in lead generation and nurture.

Crafting an effective conversion strategy involves understanding the customer's journey, addressing potential objections, and providing the necessary incentives to prompt action. Whether it's a limited-time offer, a special discount, or exclusive access to premium content, businesses use various tactics to create a sense of urgency and value that propels leads to convert.

Synergy in Action: Integrating the Three Pillars

The true power of these pillars lies not in isolation but in their integration. A seamless flow from lead generation to nurture and, finally, conversion creates a holistic social media marketing strategy. Each piece of content, every engagement, and every call to action is strategically aligned with these pillars, ensuring that businesses not only attract and engage their audience but guide them through a purposeful journey that culminates in meaningful actions.

As we delve deeper into this book, we will explore practical techniques, case studies, and actionable insights to help you master the art of Lead Generation, Lead Nurture, and Lead Conversion. Get ready to witness the synergy of these pillars as they propel your social media presence to new heights and drive tangible results for your business.

Setting the Stage: Understanding Your Audience

In the realm of social media marketing, understanding your audience is not just a preliminary step; it's the cornerstone upon which your entire strategy is built. Setting the stage begins with a deep dive into the psyche of your potential customers, and the more intimately you comprehend their needs, preferences, and behaviors, the more effectively you can tailor your content and engagement strategies.

Identifying Your Target Audience: Precision Over Reach

Identifying your target audience is not about casting a wide net; it's about precision. Social media platforms offer an incredible array of tools and analytics that allow businesses to pinpoint and define their target demographic with remarkable accuracy. It goes beyond broad categories like age and gender; it delves into interests, online behavior, and even the specific challenges or aspirations that resonate with your potential customers.

In this era of personalization, one-size-fits-all marketing is outdated. Businesses that resonate most powerfully with their audience are those that can speak directly to the individual. Through targeted advertisements, insightful content creation, and strategic engagement, you can ensure that your message reaches the right ears – those most likely to not only hear it but respond to it.

Creating Audience Personas: Bringing Data to Life

To truly understand your audience, it often helps to create audience personas. These are fictional, detailed representations of your ideal customers based on real data and insights. Each persona embodies a segment of your audience and includes demographic details, interests, pain points, and even behavioral traits. By personifying your audience, you're better equipped to tailor your messaging and content to resonate on a personal level.

Consider a business selling fitness apparel. Their audience personas might include the "Fitness Enthusiast," the "Casual Exerciser," and the "Aspiring Fitness Novice." Each persona requires a unique approach – the enthusiast may respond well to advanced workout tips, while the novice might appreciate beginner-friendly routines. Crafting content with these personas in mind ensures that your messaging speaks directly to the specific needs and aspirations of each segment.

Listening and Adapting: The Iterative Process

Understanding your audience is not a static achievement but an ongoing process. Social media provides a dynamic arena where trends, preferences, and behaviors can shift rapidly. Regularly listening to your audience involves monitoring social media interactions, analyzing feedback, and adapting your strategies accordingly.

Tools like social media analytics, surveys, and engagement metrics are invaluable in this iterative process. They allow you to measure the effectiveness of your content, identify patterns in audience behavior, and fine-tune your approach based on real-time data. By staying attuned to your audience's evolving needs, you can ensure that your social media presence remains relevant and resonant.

Connecting on a Human Level: Beyond Metrics

While metrics and analytics provide crucial insights, it's essential not to lose sight of the human aspect of your audience. Beyond the data points lie real individuals with emotions, aspirations, and challenges. Engaging with your audience on a personal level fosters a sense of connection and community. Responding to comments, initiating conversations, and showing genuine interest in your audience's experiences create a bond that transcends the digital realm.

In the chapters ahead, we'll explore actionable strategies and case studies to help you refine and deepen your understanding of your audience. Get ready to transform your social media presence from a broadcast channel to a conversation hub, where your content resonates profoundly with the individuals who matter most to your business.

Creating a Memorable Brand Image

In the ever-evolving landscape of social media, creating a memorable brand image is not just about standing out; it's about leaving an indelible mark in the hearts and minds of your audience. Your brand image is the essence of who you are as a business, and in the vast sea of content, a distinctive and resonant brand is what sets you apart and forges a lasting connection with your audience.

Visual Consistency: Crafting a Cohesive Identity

At the heart of a memorable brand image lies visual consistency. From your logo to your color palette and imagery, every element should harmonize to convey a cohesive identity. Social media platforms offer businesses a visual playground, allowing for creative expression and brand representation. Ensuring that your visuals align with your brand's personality and values creates a visual signature that your audience can recognize instantly.

Consider the iconic golden arches of McDonald's or the swoosh of Nike. These visuals have become synonymous with the brands they represent. Consistency in visuals not only reinforces brand recall but also establishes a sense of trust and reliability. When your audience sees a post or an ad, they should instantly recognize it as uniquely yours.

Authentic Storytelling: Beyond Products and Services

While visuals are a crucial aspect, a memorable brand image transcends aesthetics. It's about storytelling that resonates with your audience on a human level. Authenticity has become a cornerstone in brand building, and social media provides a platform to tell your brand's story in a compelling and genuine manner.

Share the journey of your brand – the challenges, triumphs, and the values that drive you. Highlight the faces behind the scenes, giving a human touch to your brand. Whether it's a startup born out of passion or a legacy business with decades of history, weaving these narratives into your content fosters a connection with your audience. Authentic storytelling creates a memorable brand image by evoking emotions and building a narrative that goes beyond products and services.

Engagement and Responsiveness: Building Relationships

A memorable brand image is not just about broadcasting messages; it's about engaging in meaningful conversations. Social media is a two-way street, and businesses that actively participate in the dialogue cultivate a brand image that values its audience. Responding to comments, addressing concerns, and acknowledging positive interactions contribute to building a responsive and approachable brand.

Take Wendy's Twitter account, for example. Their witty and humorous responses to customer tweets have not only garnered attention but have contributed to shaping their brand image as approachable and fun. Engaging with your audience in a genuine and timely manner transforms your brand from a distant entity to a relatable companion on the digital journey.

Consistent Tone and Messaging: Establishing Brand Voice

Your brand's voice is its unique personality expressed through words. Consistency in tone and messaging across all social media channels reinforces your brand identity. Whether your brand is playful, informative, or inspiring, the language you use should reflect this consistently.

Developing a style guide for your brand's communication ensures that every piece of content, from captions to blog posts, adheres to a predefined voice. This consistency not only helps in brand recall but also builds trust. Your audience comes to expect a certain experience from your brand, and meeting those expectations creates a lasting and positive impression.

Memorable Moments: Creating Shareable Experiences

In the age of viral content, creating memorable moments is a powerful strategy for brand building. Whether it's a clever campaign, a heartwarming story, or an interactive challenge, moments that resonate with your audience become shareable experiences. Encourage user-generated content, run contests, and tap into the power of shared experiences to amplify your brand's reach.

In conclusion, creating a memorable brand image on social media is an art that combines visual aesthetics, authentic storytelling, engagement, consistent messaging, and shareable experiences. As we navigate the chapters ahead, we'll delve deeper into practical strategies and case studies to help you craft a brand image that not only stands out but leaves an enduring imprint in the minds of your audience. Get ready to elevate your brand presence and make every interaction a memorable moment.

Crafting Compelling Content: The Heart of Social Synergy

Crafting compelling content is the beating heart of social media synergy, where the intersection of creativity and strategy forms the bridge between businesses and their audiences. At the core of this synergy lies the art of storytelling—a powerful tool that transcends mere marketing and weaves narratives that resonate with the emotions and experiences of your audience.

The Art of Storytelling: Beyond Information to Connection

In the noisy landscape of social media, storytelling stands out as a beacon that captures attention and fosters connection. It's more than presenting information; it's about creating an experience that resonates with your audience on a profound level. A well-told story has the ability to evoke emotions, build empathy, and leave a lasting impression.

Building a Story Inventory is a strategic approach to ensure a continuous flow of engaging narratives.

This inventory consists of diverse stories that showcase different facets of your brand. It could include your origin story, customer testimonials, behind-the-scenes glimpses, success stories, or even challenges you've overcome. Each story serves a unique purpose, contributing to the rich tapestry of your brand's narrative.

Know Your Stories: Origin, Transformation, and Triumph

Your story inventory should encompass various types of stories, each designed to elicit specific emotional responses from your audience. The Origin Story, for instance, delves into the roots of your business—how it began, the challenges faced, and the vision that propelled its inception. This narrative connects your audience with the authenticity and passion that birthed your brand.

Transformation stories resonate with the journey of growth and evolution. Whether it's the evolution of your products, services, or the positive impact your brand has had on customers' lives, these stories showcase progress and instill a sense of optimism. Triumph stories celebrate victories, milestones, and successes, creating a narrative of accomplishment that reinforces the credibility and reliability of your brand.

Capturing the Epiphany: Creating Engaging Content

An essential element of storytelling is capturing the audience's attention through an epiphany—a moment of realization or insight that leaves a lasting impact. Crafting content with the intention to create epiphanies involves understanding your audience's pain points, aspirations, or challenges and addressing them in a way that sparks revelation.

For example, consider a fitness brand sharing a story about a customer who overcame self-doubt and achieved remarkable fitness goals. The epiphany lies in the realization that transformation is not just physical but also mental and emotional. By aligning your content with these pivotal moments, you not only engage your audience but also position your brand as a catalyst for positive change.

Strategic Storytelling: Aligning with Brand Objectives

While storytelling is an art, it's also a strategic tool that should align with your brand's objectives. Every story in your inventory should serve a purpose—whether it's building brand awareness, fostering customer loyalty, or driving conversions. Understanding the desired outcome allows you to tailor your stories to guide your audience through the customer journey.

For instance, if the goal is lead generation, a story could revolve around a customer's journey from discovering a problem (awareness) to finding a solution (consideration) and finally choosing your product or service (decision). The narrative subtly incorporates a call to action, seamlessly blending storytelling with strategic objectives.

User-Generated Stories: Amplifying Authenticity

Beyond the stories you create, tapping into user-generated content adds an authentic layer to your narrative. Encourage your audience to share their experiences, testimonials, and success stories. User-generated content not only amplifies your brand's authenticity but also builds a sense of community where customers become advocates for your brand.

In the chapters ahead, we will delve into practical techniques, examples, and case studies to help you master the art of storytelling and craft content that resonates deeply with your audience. Get ready to embark on a journey where each piece of content becomes a compelling chapter in the evolving story of your brand, creating not just engagement but lasting connections with your audience.

Balancing Fun Facts with Captivating Stories

In the dynamic landscape of social media, striking the right balance between fun facts and captivating stories is the key to creating a content strategy that engages and resonates with your audience. While fun facts provide bite-sized pieces of information that entertain and educate, captivating stories weave a narrative that connects with the emotions and experiences of your audience. The art lies in finding equilibrium, ensuring your content is not just informative but also emotionally compelling.

The Appeal of Fun Facts: Sparking Interest

Fun facts are the quick and quirky tidbits that capture attention and inject a sense of playfulness into your content. These nuggets of information, whether related to your industry, products, or even behind-the-scenes glimpses, serve as conversation starters. They have the power to pique curiosity and create a light-hearted atmosphere on your social media platforms.

Consider a beauty brand sharing a fun fact about the origins of a popular skincare ingredient or a tech company revealing an amusing anecdote about the development of a groundbreaking product. Fun facts create a sense of immediacy and novelty, prompting your audience to stop scrolling and take notice. They add a touch of entertainment to your content mix, fostering engagement and building a positive association with your brand.

The Impact of Captivating Stories: Forging Emotional Connections

While fun facts are the appetizers, captivating stories form the main course of your content strategy. Stories have a unique ability to transcend information and forge emotional connections. They immerse your audience in a narrative, creating an experience that resonates on a deeper level. A well-told story can evoke emotions, inspire action, and leave a lasting impression.

For instance, a fashion brand might share the story behind a new collection, detailing the inspiration, challenges faced during the design process, and the ultimate triumph of presenting it to the world. This narrative not only showcases the products but also invites the audience into the brand's journey, fostering a sense of connection and loyalty. Captivating stories humanize your brand, making it relatable and memorable in the eyes of your audience.

Striking the Balance: Harmony in Diversity

The challenge lies in finding the equilibrium between fun facts and captivating stories. Too many fun facts may make your content feel superficial, lacking depth and emotional resonance. On the other hand, an overload of stories might come off as heavy or self-indulgent, potentially overwhelming your audience. Striking the right balance is about understanding your audience's preferences and strategically interspersing both elements within your content calendar.

An effective approach is the 80/20 rule, where 80% of your content focuses on valuable, emotionally resonant stories, and 20% comprises fun facts and lighter content. This ensures a diverse and engaging content mix that caters to different audience preferences. The stories provide substance and connection, while the fun facts inject variety and keep the content dynamic.

Building a Narrative Ecosystem: Integrating Fun Facts and Stories

To maximize impact, consider integrating fun facts into your storytelling strategy. Instead of presenting facts in isolation, embed them within narratives. For example, a fitness brand could share a fun fact about the benefits of a particular exercise, seamlessly leading into a success story of a customer who transformed their fitness journey using that exercise. This integration adds an educational layer to your stories, making them informative and engaging simultaneously.

In conclusion, the synergy between fun facts and captivating stories is the cornerstone of a well-rounded social media content strategy. Strive to entertain, educate, and emotionally connect with your audience by maintaining a harmonious balance. As we navigate through the chapters ahead, we will explore practical techniques, examples, and case studies to help you master this delicate equilibrium and create content that leaves a lasting impact on your audience. Get ready to weave a narrative ecosystem that captivates and delights.

The Power of Three: Lead Generation, Nurture, and Conversion

In the realm of social media marketing, the trinity of Lead Generation, Nurture, and Conversion stands as the powerhouse that propels businesses towards sustainable growth and success. These three pillars form an interconnected system that transforms casual observers into loyal customers. In this chapter, we'll delve into the first of this formidable trio: Lead Generation, exploring how to define and implement strategies that lay the foundation for a robust customer journey.

Defining Lead Generation: Planting Seeds for Growth

Lead Generation is the initial step in the customer acquisition process, where businesses aim to capture the interest and contact information of potential customers. These potential customers, or leads, represent individuals who have shown interest in the products or services offered. The goal is not just to amass a large quantity of leads but to attract those who are genuinely interested and likely to convert into customers.

On social media platforms, Lead Generation strategies manifest through various channels such as targeted advertisements, engaging content, and enticing offers. For instance, a beauty brand might run an Instagram ad offering a free sample in exchange for the user's email address. This interaction transforms a passive observer into an engaged lead, creating an opportunity for further nurturing and conversion.

Crafting Effective Lead Magnets: Irresistible Offers

The heart of successful Lead Generation lies in crafting irresistible lead magnets – offerings that provide tangible value to potential customers in exchange for their information. These can include free resources, exclusive discounts, or access to premium content. The key is to align the lead magnet with the target audience's needs and preferences, making it a compelling proposition.

For example, an e-learning platform could offer a free downloadable e-book on "Top Strategies for Effective Learning," catering to the needs of its audience interested in educational content. By providing valuable insights, the brand not only captures leads but also establishes itself as an authority in its niche.

Utilizing Social Media Advertising: Precision Targeting

Social media platforms offer robust advertising tools that enable businesses to precisely target their desired audience. Lead Generation Ads, for instance, allow businesses to collect user information directly within the platform, streamlining the conversion process. The effectiveness of these ads lies in their ability to reach specific demographics, interests, and behaviors, ensuring that the lead generation efforts are directed towards the most relevant audience.

Consider a fitness app running targeted Facebook ads to users interested in health and wellness. By offering a free trial or a special discount, the app entices potential users to provide their information for access. This not only generates leads but also establishes a direct connection between the brand and individuals already expressing an interest in fitness.

Optimizing Landing Pages: Seamless Transition to Nurture

A seamless transition from Lead Generation to Nurture involves optimizing landing pages. Once a user clicks on an ad or engages with a lead magnet, the landing page serves as the gateway to further interaction. Clear, compelling, and user-friendly landing pages enhance the user experience and encourage visitors to willingly share their information.

Elements such as concise forms, persuasive copy, and visually appealing design contribute to an effective landing page. It should convey the value of the offer and provide a smooth pathway for users to take the desired action. An optimized landing page ensures that the momentum built during Lead Generation is maintained, setting the stage for effective lead nurturing.

As we continue our journey through the power of three, the next chapters will unravel the intricacies of Lead Nurture and Conversion. By mastering the art of Lead Generation on social media, businesses can lay the groundwork for meaningful relationships with their audience and set the stage for transformative growth. Get ready to witness the synergistic impact of these strategies as we navigate through the social media marketing landscape.

Nurturing Your Audience with Valuable Content

In the realm of social media marketing, nurturing your audience is akin to cultivating a garden – it requires careful attention, strategic planning, and a commitment to fostering growth. Once you've successfully generated leads through compelling lead magnets and strategic advertising, the next crucial step is nurturing these leads into loyal and engaged customers. This chapter explores the art of nurturing your audience with valuable content, transforming initial interest into lasting relationships.

Understanding Lead Nurture: Cultivating Connections

Lead Nurture is the process of building and maintaining relationships with leads, guiding them through the customer journey, and providing them with the information and experiences they need to make informed decisions. It's the delicate art of moving beyond the initial point of contact to establish trust, credibility, and resonance.

At the core of effective lead nurture is the recognition that not all leads are at the same stage of the buying process. Some may be ready to make a purchase, while others are still exploring options. Tailoring your content to meet the specific needs of different segments within your audience ensures that your nurture efforts are relevant and impactful.

The Role of Valuable Content: Building Trust and Authority

Valuable content is the currency of effective lead nurture. It goes beyond promotional messages and focuses on delivering information, insights, and solutions that address the pain points and interests of your audience. Whether it's blog posts, educational videos, or insightful newsletters, valuable content serves as a bridge that connects your audience with your brand.

Consider a software company that offers a free webinar on optimizing productivity through their tool. By providing actionable tips and demonstrating the value of their product, the company not only nurtures leads interested in productivity but also positions itself as an authority in the industry. Valuable content establishes a foundation of trust, laying the groundwork for future interactions.

Segmentation and Personalization: Tailoring the Experience

One-size-fits-all content rarely resonates with diverse leads. Segmentation and personalization are key strategies in lead nurture, allowing businesses to tailor content based on the unique characteristics and behaviors of their audience segments. Understanding the specific needs, preferences, and pain points of different groups enables businesses to deliver content that feels personalized and relevant.

For example, an e-commerce brand may segment its audience into categories such as "frequent shoppers," "occasional buyers," and "new prospects." Each segment receives content that aligns with their purchasing behavior – exclusive discounts for frequent shoppers, product guides for occasional buyers, and introductory offers for new prospects. This targeted approach ensures that each lead receives content that speaks directly to their interests and stage in the customer journey.

Diversifying Content Formats: Engaging Through Variety

Variety is the spice of lead nurture. Diversifying content formats keeps your audience engaged and caters to different preferences. While blog posts are excellent for conveying detailed information, visual content such as infographics and videos can be more digestible. Webinars, podcasts, and interactive quizzes add an interactive dimension, fostering a deeper connection with your audience.

Consider a fashion brand that not only shares style guides through blog posts but also engages its audience through Instagram Stories showcasing behind-the-scenes moments. The mix of educational and entertaining content creates a well-rounded nurture experience, keeping the audience intrigued and invested.

Measuring and Iterating: The Continuous Refinement

The effectiveness of lead nurture strategies can be measured through various metrics, including engagement rates, click-through rates, and conversion rates. Regularly analyzing these metrics provides insights into what resonates with your audience and what may need adjustment. It's an ongoing process of refinement, where businesses iterate on their content strategies to align with the evolving needs and preferences of their audience.

In conclusion, nurturing your audience with valuable content is a dynamic and iterative process that requires a deep understanding of your audience segments and a commitment to delivering meaningful experiences. As we progress through the subsequent chapters, we will explore advanced lead nurture techniques, case studies, and actionable insights to help you refine your approach. Get ready to cultivate lasting relationships and witness the transformative power of effective lead nurture in the social media marketing landscape.

Converting Followers into Loyal Clients

Converting social media followers into loyal clients is the culmination of a well-executed social media marketing strategy. While generating leads and nurturing your audience lay the groundwork, the final stage of conversion is where followers transition from being intrigued observers to committed customers. This chapter explores the art and science of turning your social media following into a community of loyal clients through strategic and intentional conversion efforts.

Understanding the Conversion Phase: From Interest to Action

Conversion represents the pivotal moment when a lead takes the desired action, whether it's making a purchase, signing up for a service, or engaging in a meaningful interaction. In the context of social media marketing, converting followers into clients signifies the successful culmination of efforts in building awareness, fostering engagement, and nurturing relationships.

The conversion phase is not a one-size-fits-all endeavor. Different followers may be at various stages of readiness to make a commitment. Some may have been long-time followers who are now ready to make a purchase, while others may be recent additions to your community exploring what your brand has to offer. Tailoring your approach based on the unique characteristics of your audience segments ensures that your conversion efforts are both effective and respectful of individual preferences.

Strategic Calls to Action: Guiding the Next Step

At the heart of the conversion phase lies the strategic use of Calls to Action (CTAs). A CTA is an explicit prompt that encourages followers to take a specific action, such as making a purchase, signing up for a webinar, or contacting your business. Effectively leveraging CTAs in your social media content is essential to guide your followers seamlessly from interest to action.

For instance, a fitness brand might post a compelling testimonial from a satisfied customer, concluding with a CTA inviting followers to join a limited-time fitness challenge. The CTA serves as a bridge, providing a clear pathway for interested followers to actively participate and move closer to becoming loyal clients. Strategic placement and messaging of CTAs are crucial to ensuring they align with the context of the content and inspire immediate action.

Creating FOMO (Fear of Missing Out): Limited-Time Offers and Exclusivity

The psychology of FOMO plays a significant role in the conversion process. Creating a sense of urgency through limited-time offers, exclusive promotions, or early access to products/services taps into the innate human desire not to miss out on something valuable. Social media platforms provide an ideal space to broadcast these time-sensitive offers to your followers.

Consider a fashion brand announcing a flash sale exclusively for its Instagram followers. By emphasizing the limited duration and exclusive nature of the offer, the brand not only sparks immediate interest but also compels followers to take swift action to secure the benefits. FOMO-driven conversion strategies capitalize on the dynamic and fast-paced nature of social media platforms.

Leveraging User-Generated Content: Turning Followers into Advocates

User-Generated Content (UGC) is a powerful tool in the conversion arsenal. Encouraging your followers to share their experiences, reviews, or testimonials creates an authentic and relatable narrative around your brand. Potential clients are more likely to trust the opinions and experiences of their peers, making UGC a compelling conversion strategy.

For example, a travel agency might run a campaign encouraging followers to share their favorite vacation photos with a branded hashtag. These user-contributed images not only serve as social proof but also create a sense of community and shared experiences. Incorporating UGC into your conversion efforts transforms followers into advocates, amplifying the trust factor and facilitating the decision-making process for potential clients.

Analyzing Conversion Metrics: Fine-Tuning Strategies

In the age of data analytics, monitoring and analyzing conversion metrics is crucial for refining your strategies. Metrics such as conversion rates, click-through rates on CTAs, and customer acquisition costs provide insights into the effectiveness of your conversion efforts. Regularly assessing these metrics allows businesses to identify what resonates with their audience and make data-driven adjustments to optimize conversion rates.

In conclusion, converting social media followers into loyal clients requires a nuanced approach that combines strategic CTAs, a sense of urgency, the power of FOMO, and the authenticity of user-generated content. As we proceed through the subsequent chapters, we will explore advanced conversion tactics, case studies, and actionable insights to help you master the art of turning your social media community into a thriving base of loyal clients. Get ready to witness the transformative impact of effective conversion strategies in the dynamic landscape of social media marketing.

Tactics for Success: Landing Your Dream Clients

In the dynamic realm of social media marketing, landing your dream clients requires a strategic and intentional approach. While the journey begins with lead generation and progresses through nurturing and conversion, the pivotal role of a strong call to action (CTA) cannot be overstated. This chapter delves into the art of crafting a compelling CTA that not only invites your audience to take the next step but serves as a catalyst for establishing meaningful connections and securing dream clients.

The Power of the Strong Call to Action: Guiding the Narrative

A strong call to action is more than a mere prompt; it's a narrative guide that steers your audience towards the desired destination. Whether it's urging them to make a purchase, sign up for a webinar, or join an exclusive community, a well-crafted CTA serves as the gateway to deeper engagement. It's the bridge that transforms passive observers into active participants in your brand's story.

Consider a scenario where a business coach shares a video on LinkedIn discussing the transformative impact of their coaching services. A strong CTA at the end of the video could invite viewers to schedule a complimentary consultation to explore how they can achieve similar results. The CTA acts as an invitation, inviting the audience to transition from being inspired by the content to actively pursuing a personalized solution.

Clarity and Simplicity: The Essence of an Effective CTA

A successful CTA is characterized by its clarity and simplicity. Ambiguity can lead to hesitation, causing potential clients to navigate away without taking the desired action. Therefore, it's crucial to articulate the next steps with precision and simplicity, leaving no room for confusion.

For instance, a fitness influencer promoting a new workout program might include a CTA like "Start

Your Fitness Journey Today – Click the Link to Join Our 30-Day Challenge." This CTA clearly communicates the action to be taken (clicking the link) and the immediate benefit (joining the 30-day challenge). By keeping it clear and straightforward, the influencer enhances the likelihood of followers seamlessly transitioning from interest to active participation.

Creating a Sense of Urgency: Fostering Immediate Action

Urgency is a potent psychological trigger that can significantly impact conversion rates. Crafting a CTA that conveys a sense of urgency motivates your audience to take immediate action, fearing the possibility of missing out on a valuable opportunity.

Imagine an e-commerce brand launching a limited-time offer for its premium product. The CTA could emphasize the urgency by stating, "Exclusive Deal – Ends in 24 Hours! Secure Yours Now." This not only compels followers to act promptly but also instills a sense of exclusivity, making the offer even more enticing. By leveraging urgency in the CTA, businesses create a dynamic and responsive environment on social media.

Tailoring CTAs to Platform Dynamics: Aligning with User Behavior

Different social media platforms have distinct user behaviors and dynamics. Tailoring your CTAs to align with these nuances ensures that your message resonates effectively on each platform. What works seamlessly on Instagram might require adaptation for optimal impact on LinkedIn or Twitter.

For example, a travel agency promoting a limited-time discount may use a CTA like "Swipe Up to Book Now" on Instagram Stories due to the platform's swipe-up feature. On Twitter, the same agency might craft a tweet with a CTA such as "Book Your Dream Vacation – Check the Link in Bio." By aligning CTAs with platform-specific features, businesses maximize their reach and engagement.

Analyzing CTA Performance: Iterating for Optimization

The journey doesn't end with crafting a strong CTA; continuous analysis and optimization are vital for sustained success. Monitoring the performance of CTAs through metrics like click-through rates and conversion rates provide valuable insights into audience responsiveness. Regularly assessing these metrics allows businesses to iterate on their CTA strategies, refining them based on what resonates most effectively with their dream clients.

In conclusion, the strong call to action serves as the linchpin in the process of landing dream clients through social media marketing. By combining clarity, simplicity, urgency, and platform-specific tailoring, businesses create CTAs that not only invite their audience to take the next step but also empower them to become active participants in the brand narrative. As we navigate through the subsequent chapters, we will explore additional tactics and case studies to elevate your CTA game and optimize your journey toward landing your dream clients. Get ready to witness the transformative impact of strategic CTAs in the dynamic landscape of social media marketing.

Know, Like, Trust: Building Meaningful Connections

In the expansive realm of social media marketing, the journey from attracting an audience to converting them into loyal clients hinges on a fundamental principle: Know, Like, Trust. This trio of interconnected elements forms the bedrock of building meaningful connections with your audience, establishing a foundation of trust and credibility that transcends the digital landscape.

Know: The Introduction to Your Narrative

The first pillar, "Know," represents the introductory phase where your audience becomes acquainted with your brand. This goes beyond mere recognition; it's about offering insights into your brand's personality, values, and unique characteristics. In a world inundated with content, creating a distinctive brand identity is essential for standing out.

Imagine a skincare brand using Instagram to showcase not only its products but also behind-the-scenes glimpses of the production process, spotlighting the team, and sharing the brand's commitment to sustainability. This multifaceted approach goes beyond product promotion, allowing followers to "know" the brand on a deeper level, fostering a sense of familiarity and connection.

Like: The Emotional Connection

Moving beyond acquaintance, the second pillar, "Like," delves into the realm of emotional connection. It's about resonating with your audience on a personal level, evoking positive emotions, and cultivating a genuine affinity. Brands that successfully navigate this phase are those that align with the values, aspirations, and preferences of their audience.

Consider a fitness influencer sharing not only workout routines but also personal anecdotes, challenges, and moments of vulnerability. By being relatable and sharing authentic experiences, the influencer becomes more than a source of fitness advice; they become someone the audience genuinely "likes." This emotional connection establishes a bond that goes beyond transactional relationships.

Trust: The Cornerstone of Long-Term Relationships

Trust, the third and most critical pillar, is the cornerstone upon which long-term relationships are built. Trust goes hand in hand with reliability, consistency, and transparency. It's the culmination of consistently delivering on promises, being transparent in communications, and aligning actions with brand values.

For instance, an online course creator who consistently provides valuable free content, maintains open communication channels, and delivers high-quality courses builds trust with their audience. This trust becomes the bedrock of client relationships, influencing purchasing decisions and fostering loyalty.

The Role of Consistent Branding: A Unified Presence

Consistent branding plays a pivotal role in the Know, Like, Trust journey. From visual elements such as logos and color schemes to the tone of voice in communication, maintaining a unified brand presence across all platforms enhances recognition and fosters a cohesive brand image.

Consider a technology startup using consistent branding in its social media posts, website, and promotional materials. The recognizable color palette and logo create a cohesive visual identity, reinforcing the "Know" element. This consistency extends to messaging and interactions, contributing to the development of a brand personality that resonates with the audience's preferences, facilitating the "Like" and "Trust" phases.

Humanizing Your Brand: Behind-the-Scenes Narratives

Humanizing your brand amplifies the Know, Like, Trust dynamics. Sharing behind-the-scenes narratives, introducing team members, and showcasing the human side of your business contribute to a relatable and approachable image. In the age of digital interactions, humanizing your brand fosters a sense of connection that transcends the virtual space.

Imagine a local coffee shop using Instagram Stories to introduce the baristas, share the daily routines, and highlight the passion behind each cup of coffee. This narrative humanizes the brand, allowing followers to connect with the faces and stories behind the business, enhancing the "Like" and "Trust" components.

Navigating the Social Landscape: Tailoring to Platform Dynamics

Each social media platform comes with its own dynamics and user behaviors. Tailoring your Know, Like, Trust strategy to align with these nuances ensures optimal engagement and connection. What resonates on Instagram Stories might differ from what engages users on LinkedIn or Twitter.

For example, a fashion brand might leverage Instagram's visual-centric nature to showcase its products, using stories to unveil new collections. On LinkedIn, the same brand might share thought leadership articles about sustainable fashion, catering to a more professionally oriented audience. Tailoring content to platform dynamics enhances the effectiveness of the Know, Like, Trust journey.

Measuring Connection Metrics: Gauging Audience Sentiment

Measuring the success of the Know, Like, Trust journey involves assessing metrics that indicate audience sentiment. Engagement rates, sentiment analysis from comments and reviews, and brand mentions provide insights into how well your brand is progressing through each phase. Regularly monitoring these metrics helps businesses gauge the effectiveness of their connection-building efforts and make informed adjustments.

In conclusion, the Know, Like, Trust framework serves as a guiding compass for building meaningful connections in the realm of social media marketing. As we progress through the subsequent chapters, we will explore advanced strategies, case studies, and actionable insights to elevate your Know, Like, Trust game. Get ready to delve deeper into the art of connection-building and witness the transformative impact on your brand's relationships with its audience in the dynamic landscape of social media.

The 80/20 Rule: Striking the Right Balance in Your Content

In the dynamic landscape of social media marketing, where content is king, mastering the delicate balance between providing value and promoting your brand is a strategic art form. The 80/20 Rule, a concept widely embraced in content creation, advocates dedicating 80% of your content to providing value and only 20% to promotional elements. This chapter explores the essence of the 80/20 Rule, its application across diverse content formats, and how striking this balance enhances audience engagement and brand loyalty.

Understanding the 80/20 Rule: The Balance Equation

The 80/20 Rule, often referred to as the Pareto Principle, is a principle that asserts that, in many situations, roughly 80% of the effects come from 20% of the causes. Applied to social media content, it suggests that the majority of your content (80%) should be focused on delivering value, education, entertainment, and engagement, while a smaller portion (20%) can be allocated to promotional and brand-specific messaging.

This principle aligns with the core philosophy of social media, where users seek valuable and relevant content that resonates with their interests rather than being bombarded with overtly promotional material. Striking the right balance ensures that your brand remains a welcome presence in your audience's feeds, fostering a positive perception and long-term connection.

Providing Value: The 80% that Builds Relationships

The bulk of your content, the 80%, is the foundation for building meaningful relationships with your audience. This is where you showcase your expertise, share valuable insights, entertain, and engage. Whether it's educational blog posts, entertaining videos, or thought-provoking infographics, the primary goal is to add value to your audience's lives.

Consider a beauty brand utilizing Instagram to share skincare tips, makeup tutorials, and behind-the-scenes glimpses of product development. By consistently delivering content that enhances the audience's knowledge and provides real value, the brand becomes a go-to resource in the beauty community, fostering trust and loyalty.

Building Community: The Essence of Engagement

The 80/20 Rule is not just about the quantity of content but the quality of engagement. By focusing on content that resonates with your audience's interests, you cultivate a community around your brand. Engage with comments, encourage discussions, and create a space where your audience feels heard and valued.

For instance, a fitness brand might initiate weekly Q&A sessions on Twitter, responding to followers' inquiries about workout routines, nutrition, and wellness. This interactive approach not only contributes to the 80% value-driven content but also strengthens the sense of community, making followers more likely to embrace the brand's promotional messages when they arise.

Strategic Promotion: The 20% that Drives Action

While the majority of your content builds relationships, the 20% dedicated to promotion serves as the catalyst for action. This is where you showcase your products, services, or calls to action (CTAs). By strategically interspersing promotional content within the valuable content stream, you create a harmonious blend that encourages your audience to take the desired actions.

An e-commerce brand might leverage the 20% for announcing product launches, exclusive discounts, or limited-time offers. The key is to make these promotional messages contextual, ensuring they align with the interests and needs of your audience established through the 80% value-driven content.

Platform-Specific Adaptation: Tailoring to Audiences

Different social media platforms have distinct user behaviors and expectations. Adapting the 80/20 Rule to the dynamics of each platform ensures that your content resonates effectively. What works seamlessly on Instagram might require adjustment for optimal impact on LinkedIn or TikTok.

For instance, a travel agency might use Instagram to share breathtaking travel stories (80%) and reserve the 20% for promoting limited-time travel packages through engaging visuals. On LinkedIn, the agency might focus more on thought leadership articles, aligning with the professional context of the platform while still maintaining the 80/20 balance.

Measuring Impact: Metrics for Evaluation

Measuring the impact of the 80/20 Rule involves assessing metrics that reflect audience engagement, brand perception, and conversion rates. Metrics such as likes, shares, comments, click-through rates, and conversion rates provide insights into the effectiveness of your content strategy. Regularly analyzing these metrics empowers businesses to refine their approach, ensuring the 80/20 Rule remains an adaptive and evolving strategy.

In conclusion, the 80/20 Rule is a guiding principle that transforms content creation into a strategic endeavor. As we navigate through the subsequent chapters, we will delve into advanced strategies, case studies, and actionable insights to help you master the art of striking the right balance in your content. Get ready to refine your approach and witness the transformative impact of a harmonious content strategy on audience engagement and brand loyalty in the dynamic landscape of social media marketing.

Practical Tips for Implementing Your Strategy

Creating a robust social media presence is a cornerstone of any successful marketing strategy. In this chapter, we'll explore practical tips for implementing your strategy, focusing on building and maintaining a strong social media presence. From platform selection to content optimization, these insights will guide you in establishing a compelling brand identity, fostering engagement, and maximizing the impact of your social media efforts.

Strategic Platform Selection: Where Your Audience Resides

Choosing the right social media platforms is the initial step in creating a strong presence. Different platforms cater to diverse demographics and interests. Conduct thorough research to identify where your target audience resides and tailor your strategy accordingly.

For instance, if your business targets a younger demographic interested in visually engaging content, platforms like Instagram or TikTok may be more effective. On the other hand, B2B ventures might find LinkedIn to be a hub for professional networking and thought leadership.

Consistent Branding Across Platforms: Visual Cohesion

Consistency is key when it comes to branding across multiple platforms. From profile pictures and cover photos to color schemes and tone of voice, maintaining a cohesive visual identity fosters instant recognition. Your audience should experience a seamless transition when navigating from one platform to another.

Consider a fashion brand using the same logo, color palette, and tone of voice on Instagram, Facebook, and Pinterest. This visual cohesion reinforces the brand's identity, making it easier for followers to connect and engage across various social channels.

Optimizing Profiles: A Compelling Introduction

Your social media profiles serve as the digital face of your brand. Craft compelling and informative profiles that succinctly convey your brand's essence. Include a concise yet impactful bio, relevant contact information, and links to your website or other social channels.

For example, a fitness influencer's Twitter bio might succinctly communicate their niche, such as "Passionate about holistic wellness. Transforming lives, one workout at a time. Join the journey!" This bio provides a glimpse into the influencer's focus and invites followers to explore further.

Content Calendar and Consistency: Establishing a Rhythm

Consistency is a linchpin in maintaining a strong social media presence. Develop a content calendar outlining your posting schedule, ensuring a steady flow of engaging content. Consistency fosters anticipation, and followers are more likely to engage when they know when to expect your posts.

Whether it's daily fitness tips, weekly industry insights, or monthly product highlights, a content calendar allows you to plan strategically. Tools like social media management platforms can assist in scheduling posts, ensuring your content reaches your audience at optimal times.

Engagement Strategies: Nurturing Two-Way Conversations

Engagement is a reciprocal process. Actively engage with your audience through comments, likes, and shares. Encourage conversations by asking questions, seeking opinions, or running polls. Respond promptly to messages and comments, fostering a sense of community and connection.

For instance, a food blogger might post a recipe on Instagram and ask followers about their favorite variations. By initiating a conversation, the blogger not only gathers valuable insights but also strengthens the sense of community among followers.

Leveraging Visual Content: The Power of Imagery

Visual content holds immense sway in capturing attention on social media. Invest in high-quality visuals, including images, videos, and infographics. Tailor your visual content to align with your brand identity and evoke the desired emotional response from your audience.

Imagine a travel agency sharing stunning images of exotic destinations on Pinterest. Each image is carefully curated to convey the allure of the location, sparking wanderlust and engagement. Utilize the visual aspect of social media to tell your brand story and leave a lasting impression.

Analyzing Insights: Data-Driven Optimization

Regularly analyze social media insights to gauge the performance of your content. Platforms provide valuable metrics such as reach, engagement, and audience demographics. Use these insights to refine your strategy, emphasizing content types and posting times that resonate most with your audience.

For instance, a tech company might notice higher engagement on LinkedIn for informative articles about industry trends. Armed with this insight, they can prioritize similar content to maximize audience engagement.

In conclusion, implementing a strong social media presence requires a strategic approach encompassing platform selection, consistent branding, optimized profiles, a well-defined content calendar, engaging strategies, visually appealing content, and data-driven analysis. As we progress through subsequent chapters, we will delve into advanced tactics, case studies, and actionable insights to elevate your social media strategy. Get ready to refine your presence and witness the transformative impact of a compelling social media strategy on audience engagement and brand success in the dynamic landscape of digital marketing.

Using Intentional Calls to Action in Every Piece of Content

Intentional Calls to Action (CTAs) serve as the heartbeat of an effective social media marketing strategy. In this chapter, we'll explore the transformative impact of incorporating intentional CTAs into every piece of content. From lead generation to nurturing and conversion, a well-crafted CTA guides your audience seamlessly through the customer journey, turning casual followers into engaged clients.

The Essence of a Strong Call to Action: Guiding Your Audience

A CTA is more than a simple prompt; it's a directive that guides your audience toward a specific action. Whether it's clicking a link, subscribing to a newsletter, or making a purchase, a well-executed CTA serves as the bridge between valuable content and actionable engagement. By integrating intentional CTAs into your content, you empower your audience to take the next step, transforming passive observers into active participants.

Consider a fitness coach sharing a motivational workout video on Instagram. A compelling CTA at the end, such as "Join the 7-day fitness challenge, click the link in bio," propels interested followers to further engage with the coach's content and offerings. This intentional directive shapes the audience's journey and sets the stage for lead generation.

Strategic Placement: Where and When to Insert CTAs

Strategic placement of CTAs is pivotal in optimizing their impact. Consider the flow of your content and strategically position CTAs where they naturally align with the narrative. Whether it's within the caption, at the end of a video, or seamlessly integrated into an infographic, the goal is to make the CTA an integral part of the user experience.

For example, a beauty brand might incorporate a CTA within a tutorial video on YouTube, encouraging viewers to visit the brand's website for exclusive product bundles. By strategically placing the CTA at a point where viewers are likely to be interested in exploring related offerings, the brand maximizes the potential for lead generation.

Crafting Compelling CTAs: The Art of Persuasion

The language and tone of your CTA play a crucial role in its effectiveness. Craft compelling CTAs that resonate with your audience's desires and emotions. Utilize action verbs, create a sense of urgency, and emphasize the value they will gain by taking the specified action.

Consider an e-commerce brand offering a limited-time discount. The CTA could be phrased as "Unlock 20% off your next purchase, use code: LIMITED20 – Shop now!" This not only creates a sense of urgency but also clearly communicates the benefit, enticing followers to convert.

Aligning CTAs with Business Objectives: Lead Generation, Nurture, Conversion

Every CTA should align with specific business objectives, whether it's lead generation, lead nurture, or conversion. Tailor your CTAs to guide your audience through these stages of the customer journey seamlessly. For instance, a lead generation-focused CTA might encourage followers to download a free resource, while a conversion-oriented CTA could promote a limited-time offer.

A business coach might employ a multi-tiered CTA strategy. In a video, they may prompt viewers to download a free guide for lead generation. Subsequently, in a follow-up email, the CTA could lead to a webinar for lead nurture. Ultimately, a conversion-focused CTA might invite participants to enroll in a premium coaching program.

Leveraging Multiple Platforms: Adapting CTAs for Each Channel

Different social media platforms have unique user behaviors and features. Adapt your CTAs to align with the dynamics of each platform. For instance, on Instagram, use the "Link in bio" CTA in captions and stories. On Twitter, leverage concise CTAs within the character limit, and on YouTube, integrate clickable overlays or end screen elements for seamless user navigation.

A travel agency might encourage engagement on Instagram by asking followers to share their dream destinations in the comments. On Twitter, the CTA could direct users to a poll to vote for the next travel destination. The adaptability of CTAs across platforms enhances their relevance and impact.

Tracking and Analyzing CTA Performance: Iterative Optimization

Measuring the performance of your CTAs is paramount for ongoing optimization. Leverage analytics tools to track metrics such as click-through rates, conversion rates, and audience engagement. Analyzing these metrics provides insights into the effectiveness of your CTAs, allowing you to refine and tailor your approach.

For example, an e-commerce brand might use platform analytics to assess the performance of different CTAs in promoting a new product. If a specific CTA generates higher conversion rates, the brand can replicate its success in future campaigns.

In conclusion, intentional CTAs are the linchpin of a successful social media marketing strategy. By strategically placing compelling CTAs that align with business objectives, adapting them for diverse platforms, and continuously analyzing their performance, you create a dynamic and engaging user experience. As we progress through subsequent chapters, we will delve deeper into advanced CTA strategies, case studies, and actionable insights to elevate your approach. Get ready to witness the transformative impact of intentional CTAs on lead generation, nurture, and conversion in the dynamic landscape of social media marketing.

Building Brand Loyalty and Boosting Sales

Building brand loyalty and boosting sales are intertwined objectives achievable through strategic utilization of social media. In this chapter, we will explore how businesses can leverage the power of social media to cultivate brand loyalty and drive sales, creating a symbiotic relationship between a dedicated customer base and sustained business growth.

The Foundation: Understanding Brand Loyalty

Brand loyalty is not merely about repeat purchases; it's about fostering a deep, emotional connection between your brand and your audience. This connection transcends transactional relationships, evolving into a sense of trust, affinity, and genuine engagement. Social media serves as an invaluable tool for nurturing this connection, allowing businesses to interact with their audience in real-time, respond to feedback, and create a community around shared values.

Consider a skincare brand that actively engages with its customers on Instagram. By responding to comments, sharing user-generated content, and conducting live Q&A sessions, the brand transforms the transactional act of purchasing skincare products into a holistic experience. This engagement fosters a sense of community, making customers feel seen and valued.

Strategic Content for Brand Loyalty: Beyond Transactions

To build brand loyalty, businesses must move beyond purely promotional content and create a narrative that resonates with their audience. Social media platforms offer a space to showcase the personality, values, and ethos of a brand. Share behind-the-scenes glimpses, success stories, and relatable content that aligns with your audience's lifestyle.

A fitness apparel brand, for instance, might share user testimonials, highlight the manufacturing process, and celebrate fitness milestones within their community. By consistently delivering content that goes beyond selling products, the brand establishes itself as a companion in the customer's fitness journey, fostering loyalty beyond the point of sale.

Creating Exclusivity: VIP Treatment for Loyal Followers

Social media provides an opportunity to create a sense of exclusivity for loyal followers. Implement loyalty programs, exclusive discounts, or early access to product launches for those who actively engage with and support the brand. This not only rewards loyalty but also incentivizes ongoing engagement.

Imagine a coffee subscription service offering an exclusive "Subscriber's Choice" blend available only to members. This not only adds value to the subscription but makes subscribers feel like valued insiders, strengthening their commitment to the brand.

User-Generated Content: Turning Customers into Advocates

Encourage your audience to become part of the brand story by sharing their own experiences through user-generated content (UGC). Social media platforms are ideal for curating and showcasing UGC, transforming satisfied customers into brand advocates.

A travel agency might run a contest on Instagram, asking followers to share their favorite travel photos with a branded hashtag. By featuring these photos on the company's page, the agency not only amplifies the reach of genuine experiences but also turns customers into enthusiastic advocates, contributing to a positive brand image.

Responsive Customer Service: Turning Challenges into Opportunities

Social media is a frontline for customer service, providing an immediate channel for addressing concerns, queries, and feedback. Responsiveness is key to building trust and loyalty. Timely and empathetic responses to customer inquiries or issues demonstrate a commitment to customer satisfaction.

Consider an e-commerce brand addressing customer queries on Twitter. By acknowledging concerns publicly and swiftly resolving issues, the brand not only provides excellent customer service but also showcases transparency, earning the trust and loyalty of both the concerned customer and the wider audience.

Strategies for Boosting Sales: From Loyalty to Conversion

Brand loyalty is a powerful precursor to increased sales. Once a strong connection is established, businesses can strategically leverage social media to drive conversions. Limited-time promotions, personalized offers, and exclusive deals targeted at loyal followers can act as catalysts for increased sales.

A tech brand might announce a flash sale exclusively for their social media followers, rewarding their loyalty with discounted prices on popular products. This not only boosts sales but also strengthens the bond between the brand and its audience.

Measuring Success: Metrics for Loyalty and Sales

Measuring the success of brand loyalty and sales efforts on social media involves tracking metrics that reflect engagement, customer satisfaction, and conversion rates. Metrics such as customer retention rates, repeat purchase frequency, and the correlation between engagement and sales provide insights into the effectiveness of your strategies.

For example, an online bookstore might track how often customers who engage with their book recommendation posts on social media make subsequent purchases. By analyzing these metrics, the bookstore can refine its content strategy to further align with customer preferences, thereby boosting sales and loyalty.

In conclusion, leveraging social media for brand loyalty and sales involves a strategic fusion of engagement, exclusivity, user-generated content, responsive customer service, and conversion-focused initiatives. As we delve into subsequent chapters, we will explore advanced tactics, case studies, and actionable insights to elevate your approach. Get ready to witness the transformative impact of cultivating brand loyalty and driving sales in the dynamic landscape of social media marketing.

Achieving Sales Growth Through Strategic Content

Achieving sales growth through strategic content is a dynamic process that involves aligning your brand messaging, customer journey, and value proposition with the needs and interests of your target audience. In this chapter, we will explore how businesses can harness the power of strategic content to drive sales, create meaningful connections, and foster long-term customer relationships.

Understanding the Sales Funnel: A Roadmap for Content Strategy

Before delving into content creation, it's crucial to understand the sales funnel – the journey a potential customer takes from awareness to purchase. The sales funnel typically consists of three main stages: awareness, consideration, and decision. Each stage demands a tailored content strategy that resonates with the audience's specific needs and expectations.

In the awareness stage, businesses aim to capture attention and generate interest. Content here should be informative, engaging, and focused on addressing the pain points or desires of the target audience. For instance, a beauty brand might create blog posts or videos about skincare tips and trends to attract those exploring skincare solutions.

Moving to the consideration stage, content should provide in-depth information, comparisons, and solutions to position your brand as a viable option. A software company, for example, might produce case studies, webinars, or whitepapers showcasing the effectiveness of their product for businesses in the consideration phase.

Finally, the decision stage calls for content that nudges potential customers towards making a purchase. Offers, testimonials, and product demonstrations become crucial at this stage. An e-commerce fashion brand might leverage social media to showcase user testimonials, providing social proof and encouraging decisions to convert.

Personalization: Tailoring Content to Individual Preferences

Personalization is a key element in modern content strategies. By understanding individual preferences, businesses can deliver tailored content that resonates on a personal level. Utilize data analytics, customer behavior insights, and segmentation to create content that speaks directly to the unique needs and interests of your audience.

For instance, an online bookstore might employ personalized email campaigns recommending books based on a customer's previous purchases. This not only enhances the customer experience but also increases the likelihood of driving additional sales through targeted content.

Multi-Channel Presence: Meeting Customers Where They Are

Consumers interact with brands across various platforms and channels. A robust content strategy should encompass a multi-channel approach, ensuring consistency in messaging while adapting content formats to suit different platforms. From social media and email marketing to blogs and podcasts, meeting customers where they are enhances visibility and engagement.

Consider a fitness brand maintaining a dynamic presence on Instagram with workout videos, while also utilizing email newsletters to share in-depth articles on health and wellness. This multi-channel approach ensures the brand remains top-of-mind across diverse platforms, catering to a broader audience.

Educational Content: Empowering Customers with Knowledge

Educational content is a powerful tool for building trust and authority. By providing valuable insights, tips, and guides related to your industry or product, you position your brand as an expert and a reliable source of information. This fosters trust and confidence among potential customers.

For example, a software company specializing in project management tools might create webinars or tutorials demonstrating effective project management strategies. This educational content not only showcases the capabilities of the software but also positions the brand as a thought leader in the field.

Storytelling: Creating Emotional Connections

Storytelling remains a potent method for creating emotional connections with your audience. Craft narratives that resonate with your brand values and mission, weaving stories that captivate and inspire. Stories humanize your brand, making it relatable and memorable.

A sustainable fashion brand might share stories about the artisans behind their products, emphasizing ethical practices and the positive impact on communities. By narrating these stories through various content channels, the brand not only differentiates itself but also connects with conscious consumers on a deeper level.

Interactive Content: Engaging and Converting Simultaneously

Interactive content actively involves the audience, encouraging participation and engagement. Polls, quizzes, surveys, and interactive videos are effective tools for both capturing attention and gathering valuable insights. The more engaged the audience, the higher the likelihood of converting leads into customers.

A technology company might utilize interactive quizzes on its website to help customers determine the most suitable product based on their specific needs. This not only provides a personalized experience but also guides potential customers towards a purchasing decision.

Measuring Content Effectiveness: Analytics and Iterative Refinement

To achieve sales growth through strategic content, businesses must continually measure the effectiveness of their efforts. Utilize analytics tools to track key performance indicators (KPIs) such as click-through rates, conversion rates, and engagement metrics. Analyzing this data enables iterative refinement, allowing businesses to optimize their content strategy for maximum impact.

For instance, an e-commerce brand might analyze the performance of different product-focused blog posts. If one type of content consistently drives higher conversions, the brand can adjust its content calendar to prioritize similar topics, enhancing both engagement and sales.

In conclusion, achieving sales growth through strategic content requires a holistic approach that encompasses the entire customer journey. By understanding the sales funnel, personalizing content, maintaining a multi-channel presence, providing educational content, leveraging storytelling, incorporating interactive elements, and consistently measuring performance, businesses can create a dynamic and effective content strategy. As we progress through subsequent chapters, we will explore advanced tactics, case studies, and actionable insights to further refine and elevate your approach to strategic content for sustainable sales growth.

Conclusion

In this comprehensive journey through the intricacies of social media marketing, we've uncovered the essence of success lies in a strategic trifecta: lead generation, lead nurture, and lead conversion. Each chapter delved into actionable insights, from understanding your audience to crafting compelling content, and from nurturing relationships to landing dream clients. We explored the power of storytelling, the 80/20 rule, and practical tips for implementing a winning strategy. Additionally, we discovered the art of building brand loyalty, leveraging social media for sales growth, and achieving success through strategic content.

The three pillars—lead generation, lead nurture, and lead conversion—form the backbone of an effective social media marketing strategy. By carefully intertwining these elements, businesses can not only enhance their online presence but also forge meaningful connections with their audience. Through compelling stories, intentional calls to action, and a balance of valuable content, the path to sustainable success in the digital landscape unfolds.

As we conclude this journey, remember that social media is not merely a platform for content; it's a dynamic landscape where relationships are cultivated, brands are forged, and dreams are realized. The strategies unveiled here are not mere theories; they are blueprints for success, grounded in the principles of genuine connection and intentional engagement. So, armed with the knowledge acquired, step confidently into the realm of social media marketing, where every post, every interaction, and every story is a step closer to realizing your business aspirations.

www.ingramcontent.com/pod-product-compliance
Lightning Source LLC
Chambersburg PA
CBHW071056290526
45795CB00004B/1524